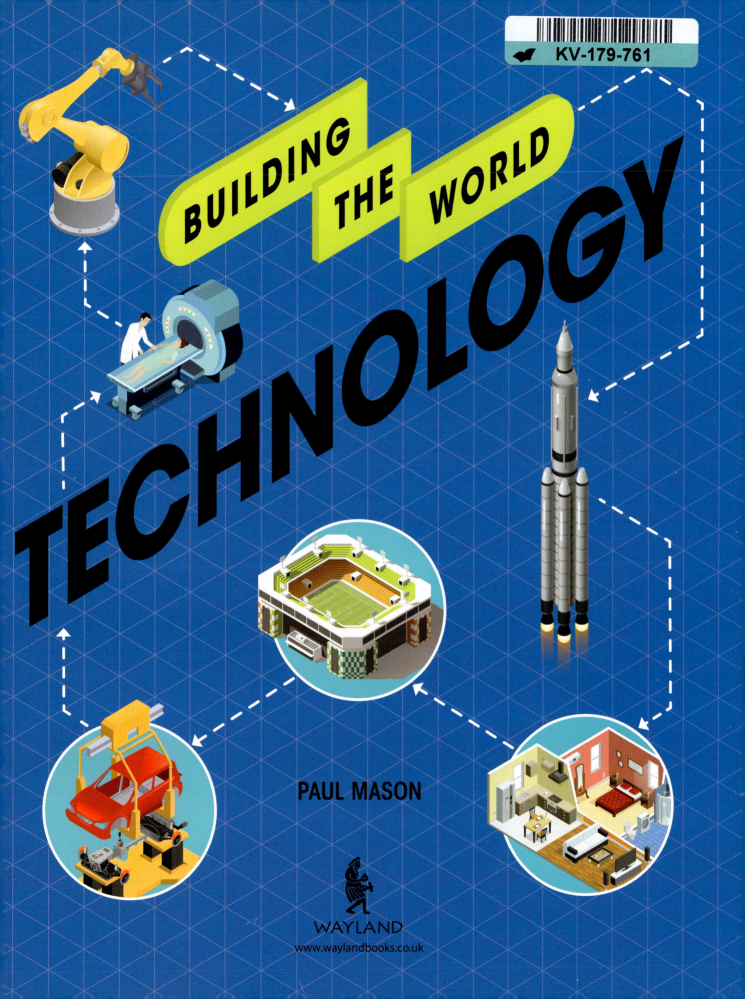

BUILDING THE WORLD

TECHNOLOGY

PAUL MASON

WAYLAND
www.waylandbooks.co.uk

First published in Great Britain
in 2019 by Wayland
Copyright © Hodder and Stoughton, 2019
All rights reserved

Senior editor: Julia Bird
Produced by Tall Tree Ltd
Editor: Jon Richards
Designer: Ed Simkins

HB ISBN: 978 1 5263 1119 1
PB ISBN: 978 1 5263 1120 7

Wayland
An imprint of Hachette Children's Group
Part of Hodder and Stoughton
Carmelite House
50 Victoria Embankment
London EC4Y 0DZ

An Hachette UK Company
www.hachette.co.uk
www.hachettechildrens.co.uk

Printed and bound in China

Picture credits: Shutterstock: 1c, 18-19 tele52,
1bl, 2t, 22l, 22b, 23tr, 23b, 31tr Dilen, 1br, 6-7,
10-11, 19t, 26b, 26-27, 27b, 32br Macrovector,
1cr, 2tl, 2c, 11cr, 14-15, 19bl, 22-23, 23br, 32bc
Sentavio, 2bl, 6bl, 7br, 32bl K-Nick, 4 Venice
Beach Photos, 5t Everett Historical, 5c
aquatarkus, 5bl vector_sign, 8l AlexLMX, 9b
MONOPOLY919, 10tl Golden Sikorka, 10bl
Mix3r, 11tr, 30 haomskii, 12 Toey Toey, 13t
EcoPrint, 13br Glynnis Jones, 14tl, 15tr, 15br
VectorPot, 15tl Inspiring, 15 cr MoonRock,
16-17 science photo, 17t nobeastsofierce, 17c
Master Video, 18cl Zern Liew, Petr Born, 18bc
aurielaki, 19t Vector_dream_team, 19br
Vladislav Ostrovskiy, 20t Stefan Holm, 20b
sportpoint, 21t Denis Faraktinov, 21r MinDof,
21b Rocksweeper, 24t Miriam Doerr Martin
Frommherz, 24br Altosvic, 25t Yullishi, NASA:
28, 29tr, 29br, Creative Commons: 25br
Richard Greenhill and Hugo Elias

The website addresses (URLs) included in this
book were valid at the time of going to press.
However, it is possible that contents or
addresses may have changed since the
publication of this book. No responsibility for
any such changes can be accepted by either
the author or the Publisher.

MIX
Paper from
responsible sources
FSC® C104740
FSC
www.fsc.org

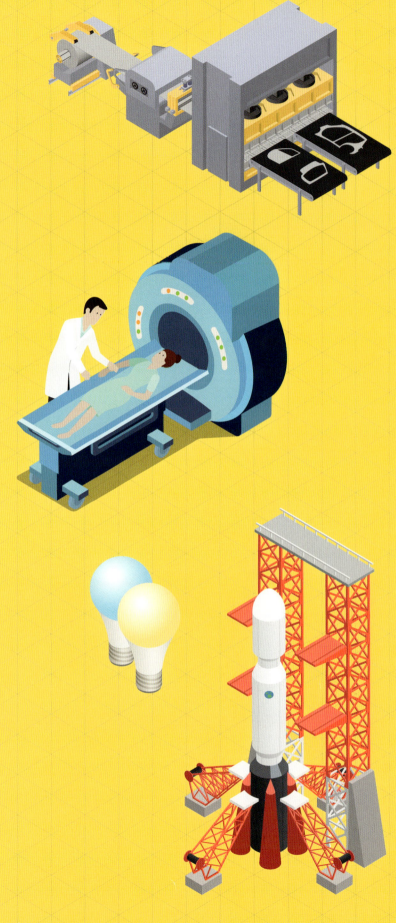

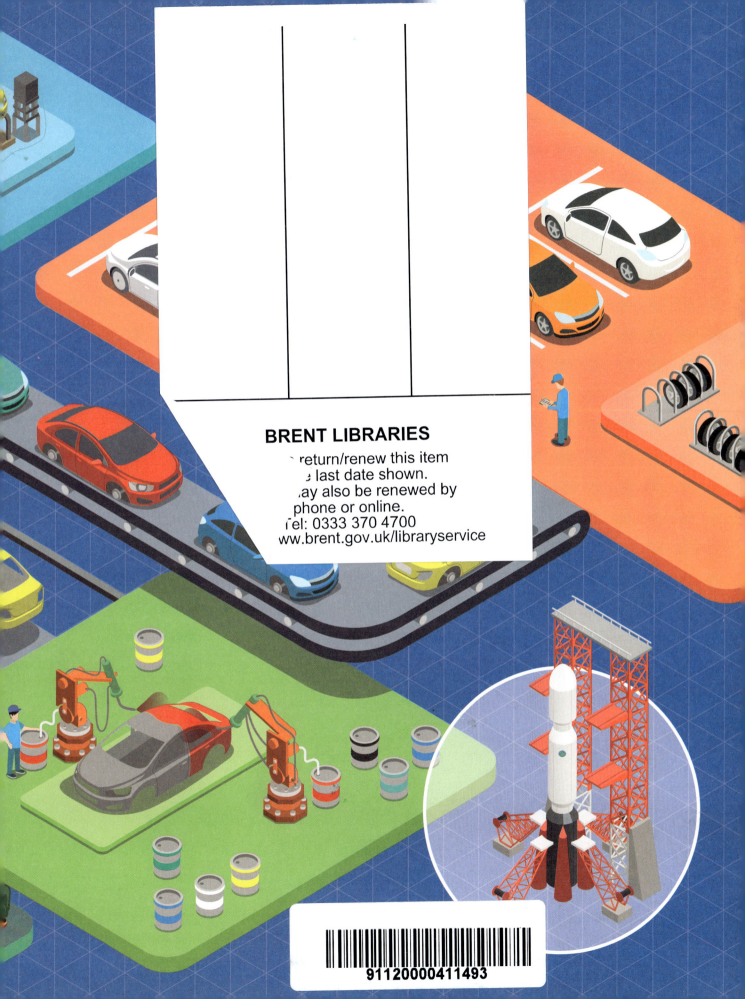

It's a techno
WORLD

Technology is scientific knowledge used in practical ways. We use technology at work, at home, at school and when we are travelling. In fact, technology is everywhere in modern life.

From simple skateboards ...

All objects rely on technology – even something as apparently simple as a skateboard. The deck needs to be as grippy as possible, with a lot of friction. The wheel bearings should spin freely, so they need low friction. The deck, trucks and wheels use technology to make the board as good as possible.

The purpose-built landscape and the smooth surface of this skatepark are designed to complement the technology of the board.

... to miniaturised marvels

Smartphones are jammed with technology, from tiny radio transmitters and receivers to miniature computer processors. They are a good example of one of the most important new technologies: miniaturisation. This is the ability to make items very small, but able to do the same job as a larger version. Without miniaturisation, smartphones, laptops, smart TVs, digital radios and other modern devices could not exist.

Early computers, such as this one from the 1940s, were much larger than today's desktop PCs. Some even needed a team of people to operate them.

The first mobile phones were much bigger than today's sleek smartphones.

Digital technology

Mobile phones and computers allow fast communication and can process huge amounts of data very quickly. The internet and mobile-phone networks allow us to talk to each other and send information from almost any spot on the planet.

In January 2018, Norway's mobile internet speeds were the fastest in the world. They were seven-and-a-half times quicker than the slowest country, Ukraine.

A modern smartphone has more computing power than the computers NASA used to send astronauts to the Moon!

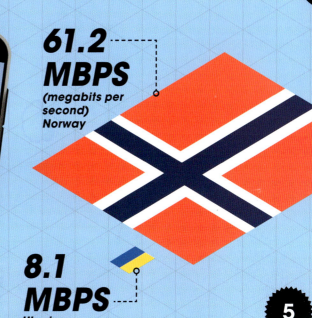

61.2 MBPS
(megabits per second)
Norway

8.1 MBPS
Ukraine

5

Home
TECHNOLOGY

Smart technology is built into many of today's homes. Often it is linked to mobile-phone apps, which let people control their heating, lighting and more.

Smart speaker

Voice control

New technology lets people control many parts of their home, such as the central heating and lights, using just their voice. A 'smart speaker' hears what they say and transmits their instructions.

Smart speakers have made life easier for many disabled or elderly people.

Lighting

Phone apps allow lights to be turned on or off while you are away. Some systems can be 'tuned' to wake you up by getting slowly brighter, for example.

Smart light bulbs

Robot vacuum cleaners can be programmed to clean the floor while you are out.

Heating and air-conditioning

Some thermostats can be controlled even when people are away, using a mobile-phone connection. A few even use artificial intelligence to learn when you usually turn them on and switch on automatically.

Smart thermostat

Who's there?

Door security

Some doorbells include a video camera linked to a mobile phone. When you are not at home, you can use the camera to see who is at the door and even talk to them.

Home entertainment

Music, TV and movies can all be linked using a wireless signal. They can play through the whole house, in every room at the same time.

Smart TV and sound system

The Internet of
THINGS

The Internet of Things is a network of devices that can communicate with each other and share data, without a human having to get involved. The Internet of Things is not only in people's homes, but also all around us.

In 2008, for the first time, *the number of devices* connected to the *Internet of Things* became bigger than the **world's population.**

GPS satellites (above) use The Internet of Things to share location information.

Transport

The Internet of Things is changing transport in many ways. Smart-parking apps can now tell you where there is a free parking space nearby. Computers use Global Positioning System (GPS) to track where a delivery van is. Sensors on streetlights can tell which roads are used most often and warn when they are likely to need repairs.

Healthcare

The Internet of Things can also be used to check on humans. Some smart watches are fitted with sensors that can monitor how a person's body is behaving. They can record data, such as heart rate, and send this to a doctor.

This smart watch is monitoring the wearer's heart rate.

15.41 billion 2015

23.14 billion 2018

Number of devices connected to the Internet of Things

35.82 billion 2021 (projected)

Agriculture

In farming, sensors can record important information about a field where crops are growing. This could include the level of sunlight, soil and air temperature, and the amount of moisture. Drones (left) can also be used to see whether crops are growing well. They relay images to computers which can work out what the crops need and trigger the use of irrigation, fertilisers or other things.

This drone is scanning a field, using infrared sensors to produce images that show the soil nutrient and water levels before a crop is planted.

Smart farming could boost sustainable food production and reduce crop waste.

Food
TECHNOLOGY

Technology is changing the way restaurants get your order to the table, ready to eat.

Delivery

Food is delivered in refrigerated trucks. Some dishes – chili or pies, for example – might be brought to the restaurant pre-prepared.

Refrigerated truck

Storing food

The first fridges used huge pieces of ice to keep their insides cool. Modern fridges use special gases to transfer heat from inside the appliance to the air outside, keeping the food nice and cool.

Refrigerators' low temperatures stop bacteria from feeding on the food and making it go rotten.

Hygiene

Keeping a kitchen and restaurant clean is very important to prevent customers getting ill. The latest chemical cleaners are designed to kill nearly all types of bacteria that could live on work surfaces and contaminate food.

Payment

Today, most people use a bank card to pay for their food. The card machine checks with their bank how much money they have and approves the payment.

Contactless payment

When an order is ready, the waiter gets a reminder to come and collect it from the kitchen.

Tablet

Ordering

In many restaurants the waiters now carry tablets that are linked to the kitchen. The table number and order are sent straight to the cooks.

Cooker

Cooking

Some modern cookers are fitted with special sensors that will tell you how long and at what temperature different foods have to be cooked so that they are safe to eat.

Food in the FUTURE

The world's population is getting bigger, making it harder to produce enough food for everyone. There may soon not be enough land or water to grow crops and raise livestock. Technology is finding ways to help.

Vertical farming

Growing crops in water instead of soil is called hydroponics. Nutrients are added to the water. Using hydroponics means crops do not have to be grown at ground level. Instead, vertical farming can be used, with 'fields' (which are actually tanks of water) stacked on top of each other. The same water can be used again and again, so the crops use less water overall.

Vertical farming using hydroponics can produce **up** **to five times** as much food from the same area of land.

This hydroponic farm is growing strawberries in tanks of water.

Alternatives to beef

Producing meat, particularly beef, uses a lot of water and land. Meat substitutes have been developed, based on legumes (plants with seed pods such as peas, chickpeas and lentils), which can be used to make different meals and offer a more sustainable, healthier dietary choice.

Cows burp and fart out a lot of methane gas, which is one of the causes of global warming.

Another alternative to beef is insects. Insects grow quickly, so insect farms might one day produce a lot of food. **Spaghetti bolognese with grasshopper, anyone?**

GM food

GM is short for genetically modified. GM seeds have had their genes changed by scientists. The changes usually make the plants more resistant to diseases or insects. This means more of them survive, and the quantity of plants that can be harvested from a piece of land becomes higher.

Many people dislike the idea of GM food and object to it being grown, because it could affect other species in the environment.

Between 2003 and 2017, the area covered by **GM crops** around the world increased by almost **three times.**

13

Medical
TECHNOLOGY

Some of the world's newest tech can be found in hospitals. Improvements in medical technology are one reason why people in many countries are living longer than ever before.

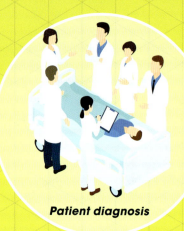

Patient diagnosis

Diagnosis

Doctors use blood tests, scans and other technology to diagnose what is wrong with someone. This is the first step to helping the patient recover.

Test analysis

Patients' blood contains clues to what is wrong with them. It can be analysed by technicians with microscopes or by computers.

Physical therapy

Sometimes, physical therapy (also called physiotherapy) is the best way to recover from an injury. Technology such as running machines may be used.

Running machine

Micro surgery

Keyhole surgery uses a small cut to thread a tiny camera inside the patient. Other cuts are made for scalpels and other operating tools to go through.

Keyhole surgery

Treatment

New drugs are being developed all the time. Computers are often used to identify the ones that work best. They can do this more quickly than humans.

Once an illness has been identified, doctors can prescribe drugs to help the patient recover.

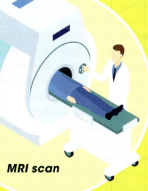

MRI scan

Seeing inside the body

MRI scanners make an image of the inside of someone's body. The image is then shown on a computer screen.

Future
HEALTH

Healthcare technology is constantly changing. In ten years' time, some radical new treatments could be available. Here are some of the biggest in development.

Gene therapy

A gene is part of a code in our bodies that carries the plan for how we grow. We get genes from each of our parents. Sometimes, the code contains a fault that causes disease, for example becoming blind or developing cancer. Scientists can use gene therapy to treat these diseases. It changes people's genes so that the diseases do not appear in the first place.

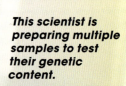

This scientist is preparing multiple samples to test their genetic content.

In 1989, the first **gene therapy trial** happened. In 2015, **163** different trials began. In total, **by the end of 2015** there had been **2,334 gene therapy trials.**

Tiny technology

Nanobots are tiny devices that can travel along blood vessels, delivering drugs exactly where they are needed. These machines measure just millionths of a metre across and are too small to see with the naked eye. Nanobots have successfully treated cancer in mice, and, one day, they could be used to treat humans as well.

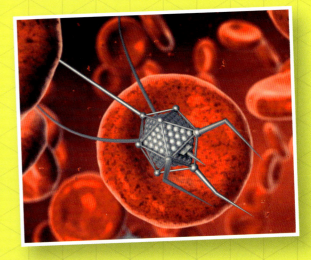

Nanobots could be used to identify potentially harmful cells, such as cancer cells, and destroy them. This artwork shows a nanobot attaching itself to a red blood cell in the bloodstream.

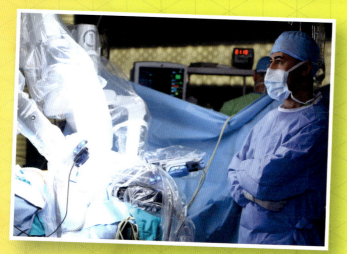

This remote-controlled robot is performing surgery. A surgeon remains on hand in case anything goes wrong.

5G surgery

Over the next few years, the next generation of mobile phone technology, known as 5G, is being established in various countries around the world. Robots are already able to perform operations under the remote control of a surgeon. Using a 5G network, the surgeon could control the robot from another city or even another country.

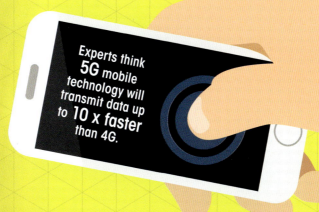

Experts think 5G mobile technology will transmit data up to 10 x faster than 4G.

Sports
TECHNOLOGY

In the last few years, new technology has helped athletes improve their fitness and coaches analyse technique. Referees also use technology to help them make the correct decisions.

Playing surfaces

Many sports used to be played only on grass. Today, artificial grass and hybrid surfaces (which mix different coverings) allow play in all weather.

Artificial grass

Running shoes for the latest tracks have short, ceramic spikes for grip. The spikes weigh 33 per cent as much as older steel ones.

Running track

Track technology

Running tracks are designed for grip and shock absorption. The newest tracks have a thin, solid layer on top for grip. Beneath this is a shock-absorbing layer.

Training and coaching

Coaches can now video an athlete's performance, then play it back in slow motion. This makes it easier to spot problems with technique.

Video coaching

Video refereeing

In football, computers can check whether or not a ball has crossed the goal line. A video assistant referee (VAR) also reviews match footage to make sure the right decisions are made. In tennis and cricket, computers work out whether the ball has touched a line or the batter's leg.

Player performance

Wearable devices can transmit information about things such as an athlete's heart rate, speed, temperature and how far they have run, swum or cycled. Coaches can then use this information to see how an athlete can improve their performance.

Wearable device

Timing

Electronic timing systems now record exactly when a swimmer touches the end of the pool, or a runner crosses the finish line.

Fitness through
TECHNOLOGY

The latest sports science and technology are not only for top sports stars. New devices and equipment can help anyone get fitter.

Scientists know that muscles work better when they are warm. Open-water swimmers wear clothes designed to keep them warm for as long as possible, even in chilly water.

Compression clothing includes tight-fitting socks and tights that squeeze the leg muscles.

Clothing technology

Some scientists think that compressing muscles while exercising increases the amount of oxygen the muscles get. With more oxygen, the muscles are able to work harder. Waste products are also removed more efficiently so that athletes feel less sore once they have finished exercising. As a result, 'compression clothing' has been developed for runners, swimmers and other athletes.

Data crunching

Modern mobile phones, apps and wearable devices can record all sorts of information about people exercising. Computers can then use this data to calculate when and how hard people should train, when to rest, what to eat and even the best time to go to sleep and wake up.

A modern smart watch records the number of steps a person has taken and how far they have travelled.

Food, drink and clothing

Technologists know more than ever before about how exercise affects people's bodies. They have created special food and drink that supply the body with extra nutrients that will make it work faster or for longer. Compression wear, UV protection and sweat-wicking fabrics, which draw moisture away from the body, are just some of the advancements in fitness clothing.

Equipment

Modern sports equipment is designed using scientific principles. One example is the fight against the force called air resistance. Scientists know that objects with aerodynamic shapes experience lower air resistance and so it takes less energy to move them forwards.

Wind tunnels are used to find the most aerodynamic shape possible in high-speed sports, such as cycling.

Robot
TECHNOLOGY

Robots are machines that carry out work for us. Today's technology means robots can do more complicated jobs than ever before. For example, robots now do much of the work making cars, trucks and motorbikes.

Computer control

The whole production process is designed and controlled using computers. Humans monitor what is happening, in case something goes wrong.

Programming

Body panels

First, robots cut sheets of metal to an exact outline. Then they bend these to make the 3D shape of a body panel.

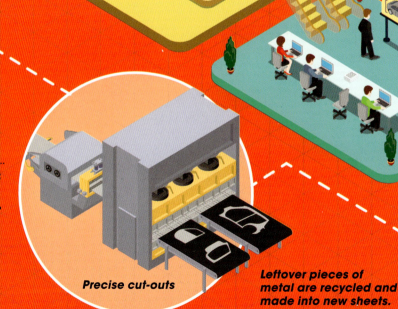

Precise cut-outs

Leftover pieces of metal are recycled and made into new sheets.

Final checks

After final checks by a human tester, the car is driven out of the factory, ready to be delivered to its new owner.

Body and engine

The car body is fitted to the engine. Final parts, such as wheels, seats and inside panels, are added by both robots and humans.

Fitting final parts

Painting

The car is painted by a robot programed to know exactly where and how much paint should be applied.

Painting

Welding

The body panels are held in position, and then joined by robot arms with spot-welding tips. The car is beginning to take shape.

Welding parts

Sensors allow robots to be exact and make it safe for humans to work nearby.

Robots of tomorrow –
TODAY

Today, robot technology has moved beyond the production line and into hospitals, the armed forces and even homes.

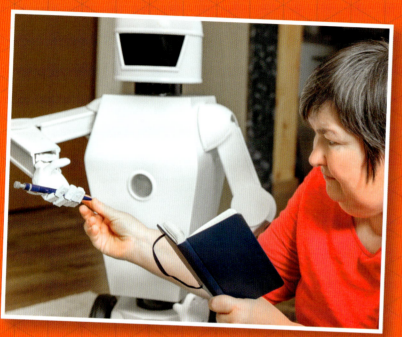

Robot healthcare

Healthcare robots are already in operation in some hospitals and homes around the world. They are used to deliver drugs, provide basic care, such as help with eating, and even help move frail patients from a wheelchair to a bed or bath. With the increasing number of elderly people, robots may well play a vital part in looking after old people.

The latest robots can read people's emotions so that they can adapt to patients' needs and only help when required.

By 2050, **the number of old people** in the world will have **doubled**.

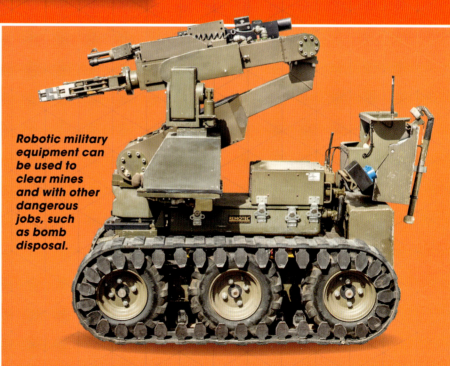

Robotic military equipment can be used to clear mines and with other dangerous jobs, such as bomb disposal.

Between *2010* and *2017*, the number of

manufacturing robots
grew by:

7%
in the Americas

5%
in Europe

9%
in Asia

The latest robots are able to keep children entertained while their parents are busy.

Smart pets

Several companies have developed robot pets. Some use artificial intelligence to learn about their owners. They can recognise faces, remember names and act excited to see you – just like a puppy does. The robots even know when they need a recharge, and head off to their charging station without being told.

Humanoid robots

Scientists are now trying to develop robots that have physical human features. These can range from robotic body parts, such as hands and feet, that can be used to replace missing or damaged limbs, to entire humanoid robots that can act as guides or companions.

Military robots

Robots are able to carry out dangerous jobs to save humans getting into danger. Military robots can deal with unexploded devices, while human soldiers operate them from a safe distance. Special, four-legged robots are also being developed that can carry important supplies to front line positions. They can cross any terrain and cover long distances, even under fire.

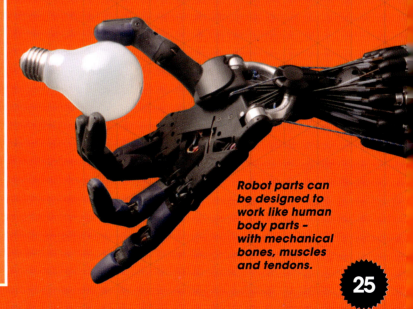

Robot parts can be designed to work like human body parts – with mechanical bones, muscles and tendons.

Rocket
POWER!

Since the launch of the first satellite in 1957, rockets have been carrying more and more advanced vehicles out into space. These spacecraft have included probes, GPS satellites and even whole space stations.

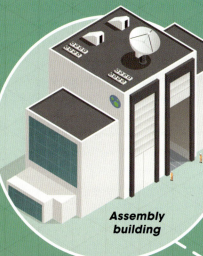

Assembly building

Assembly

Large rockets are assembled in huge, tall buildings, alongside the launch tower and launchpad.

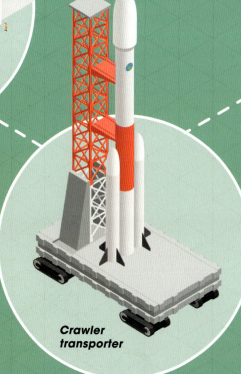

Crawler transporter

Moving a rocket

A 'crawler transporter' moves the rocket to the launch site. These huge crawlers can measure 40 m long, but they only travel at about 1.5 km/h.

Mission Control

The launch is coordinated from a mission control centre. Special devices record what is happening aboard the rocket and transmit this information back to the mission control centre via a communications dish.

Communications dish

New rockets with reusable first-stage boosters are being developed. They can travel back to Earth and land safely.

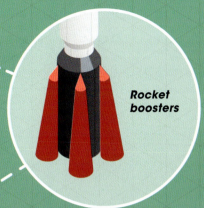

Rocket boosters

Booster stages

Some rockets fire their engines in stages. The first stage propels the rocket out of the atmosphere. It is dumped, then a second stage fires the rocket on.

Launch tower

The launch tower supports the rocket until it starts to fire. Then its attachments automatically let go, leaving the rocket free to blast off.

Launch tower

On the launchpad, the rocket is connected to a launch tower, or service structure. This allows engineers to carry out safety checks before launch.

Technology in SPACE

We use rockets to send satellites, supplies and people into space. Over the years, these vehicles have become more advanced, allowing us to explore ever more distant parts of space.

Between January 1994 and March 1995, Russian cosmonaut **Valery Polyakov** set the record of nearly **438 consecutive days in space** while on board the Mir space station.

Space stations

The International Space Station (ISS) is the biggest object ever built in space. It is a space laboratory where scientists carry out experiments to find out the effects of living in space on plants and animals. The station's technology includes solar power, water recycling and a system that makes breathable oxygen from water.

When astronauts return to Earth from the ISS, they travel in a Soyuz space module.

A Soyuz capsule undocking from the ISS.

Space exploration

Technology is allowing us to explore space in new ways. The new Orion spacecraft has been designed to transport humans further into space than ever before. It will be equipped with new breathing systems, developed from those on board the ISS. Orion will have a small power unit, communication systems and special shielding and materials to protect people from heat, damage and radiation.

NASA's Orion spacecraft is designed to carry humans to Mars.

Earth

Distance to Moon = 384,400 km

Moon

Distance to Mars = 54.6 million km

Mars

Small satellites

Satellite technology is improving all the time. Some of the biggest developments have been made possible through miniaturisation (see p.5). This has allowed satellites to become smaller (which makes it cheaper to send them into space) or to pack in more technology. New miniature satellites range in size from a loaf of bread to a small washing machine.

NASA's ultra-compact Cyclone Global Navigation Satellite System studies hurricanes to help improve weather forecasts.

Technology
WORDS

AERODYNAMIC
An object that is shaped so that it produces little air resistance.

APP
Short for application, this is a piece of computer software that has been written to do a particular job.

ARTIFICIAL INTELLIGENCE
The ability of computer systems to do activities usually done by humans.

ATMOSPHERE
The layer of gases surrounding Earth or another planet.

BACTERIA
Tiny single-celled life forms that are too small to see but grow all around us.

BLOOD VESSEL
A tube inside the human body that carries blood.

CERAMIC
A type of clay that becomes hard when heated and allowed to cool down.

COMPUTER PROCESSOR
Also called the 'central processing unit', the processor is the part of a computer that does its most basic functions, such as arithmetic.

DATA
Facts and numbers that have been collected for a special purpose.

DRONE
A robotic aircraft that does not have a human pilot.

FRICTION
A force that slows down movement, caused when one surface rubs against another.

GENE
The chemical code inside living things that carries the plan for how they will grow.

GRAVITY
A pulling force that attracts one object to another. The size of the force increases with the mass of the object.

GPS
Short for Global Positioning System, this uses satellites and radio signals for navigation anywhere on Earth.

IRRIGATION
Adding water to crops.

MINIATURISATION
Making items very small, but able to do the same job as a larger version.

NUTRIENT
A substance that is needed to stay healthy.

RADIATION
A form of energy that moves through space carried by waves or particles.

SATELLITE
An object that orbits another object in space. Satellites can be natural, like the Moon, or artificial, such as a communications satellite.

SENSOR
A device that measures physical things.

SPOT WELDING
Creating high temperature in a particular spot, so that two pieces of metal melt together.

TECHNICIAN
An expert in the practical uses of science.

TELEMETRIC
Describes a device that records information, then transmits it by radio.

Finding out more

PLACES TO VISIT

THE NATIONAL MUSEUM OF COMPUTING
BLOCK H, BLETCHLEY PARK
MILTON KEYNES
MK3 6EB
Open on Thursday, Saturday and Sunday afternoons, but
with guided tours at other times, this is a great place to see
how miniaturisation has changed the size of computers.
WEBSITE: TNMOC.ORG

MUSEUM OF TECHNOLOGY
THROCKENHOLT FARM
OLD SOUTH EAU BANK
SPALDING
LINCOLNSHIRE
PE12 0QR
The second part of the museum's name is 'The History of
Gadgets and Gizmos'; this is the place to discover the
story of small things like telephones, cameras and TVs.
WEBSITE: MUSEUMOFTECHNOLOGY.ORG.UK

CAMBRIDGE MUSEUM OF TECHNOLOGY
THE OLD PUMPING STATION
CHEDDARS LANE
CAMBRIDGE
CB5 8LD
Reopened in 2019 after improvements, this is a
museum of old industrial technology, in an impressive
building that was once a sewage works.
WEBSITE: MUSEUMOFTECHNOLOGY.COM

THINKTANK SCIENCE MUSEUM
MILLENNIUM POINT
CURZON STREET
BIRMINGHAM
B4 7XG
Not only science, but also technology can be found here. There are
more than 200 hands-on displays that let you see for yourself how
things work. Top pick for anyone interested in planes or the Battle of
Britain has to be the Spitfire Gallery. The old motorbikes and cars
are pretty cool too, though.
WEBSITE: BIRMINGHAMMUSEUMS.ORG.UK/THINKTANK

BOOKS TO READ

INFOGRAPHIC HOW IT WORKS: TODAY'S TECHNOLOGY
JON RICHARDS AND ED SIMKINS (WAYLAND, 2019)
Step-by-step infographics explain how the biggest technologies
of today work, in a way that you'll find easy to read and hard to
put down.

THE TECH-HEAD GUIDE TO DRONES AND ***THE TECH-HEAD GUIDE
TO ARTIFICIAL INTELLIGENCE***
WILLIAM POTTER (WAYLAND, 2019)
These are guides to two technologies that are getting more
important every year.

Technology
INDEX